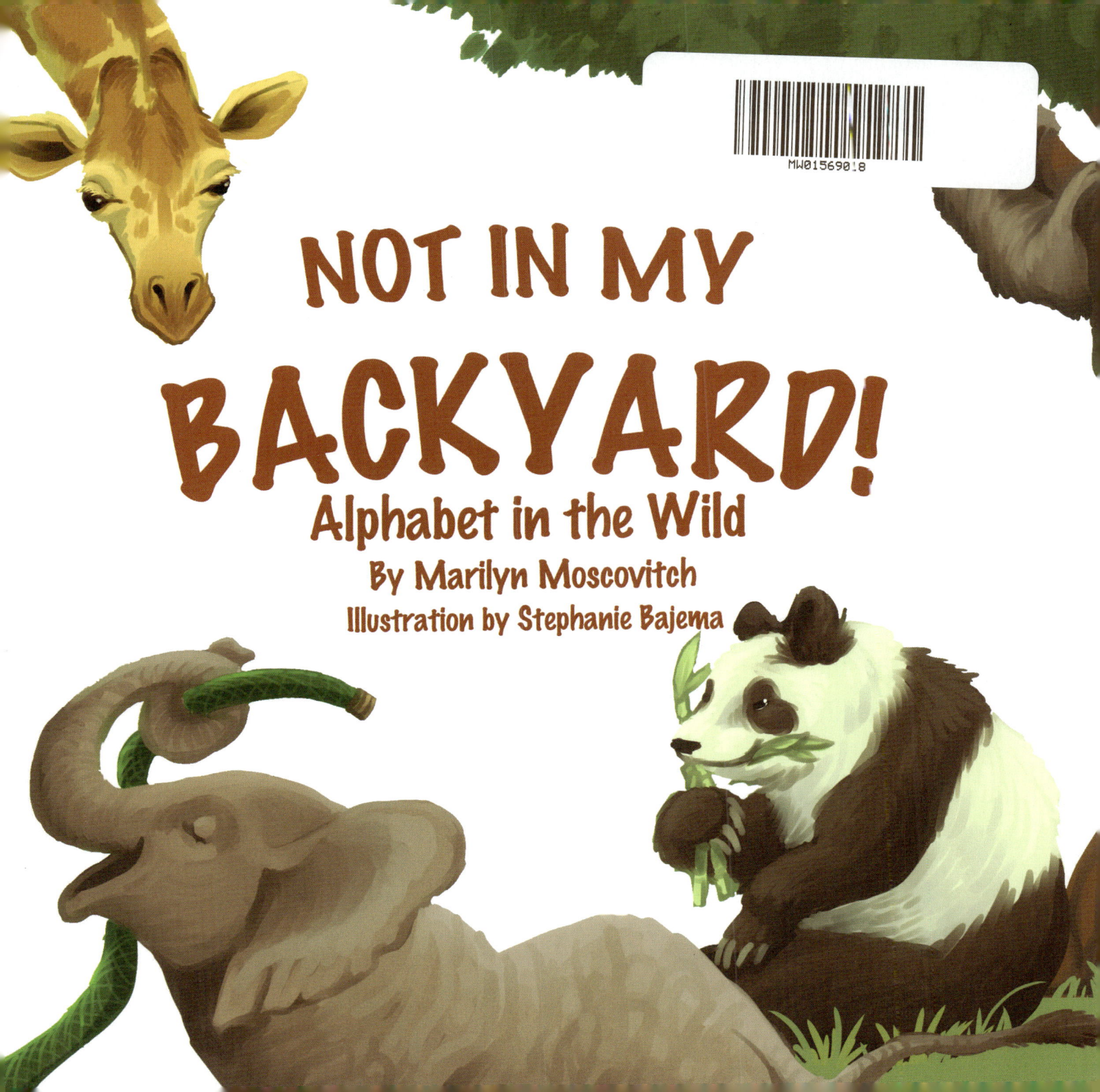

Published in 2014 by Crafty Canuck Inc.

http://shop.craftycanuck.com
www.craftycanuck.com

Copyright © 2013 by Crafty Canuck Inc. & Marilyn Moscovitch

All rights reserved. No part of this publication may be reproduced, stored in a retrieval system or transmitted, in any form or by any means, electronic, mechanical, photocopying, recording, or otherwise, without the written prior permission of the author.

Note for Librarians: A cataloguing record for this book is available from Library and Archives Canada at www.collectionscanada.ca/amicus/index-e.html

ISBN: 978-1-927471-10-4

Printed in the USA.

Written by Marilyn Moscovitch.
Illustrations by Stephanie Bajema.
Edited by Isabelle M. Eaton.

Aa Bb Cc Dd Ee Ff Gg Hh Ii Jj Kk Ll Mm

Twenty—six letters, in our alphabet.
Put side by side, now we're all set.
Each letter's special, an animal per one.
Okay, let's get started! This will be fun!

While you are reading, look carefully.
Animals or letters are hiding, you see.
Behind a large rock, maybe in a stream.
Perhaps you'll find one beneath a moonbeam.

Nn Oo Pp Qq Rr Ss Tt Uu Vv Ww Xx Yy Zz

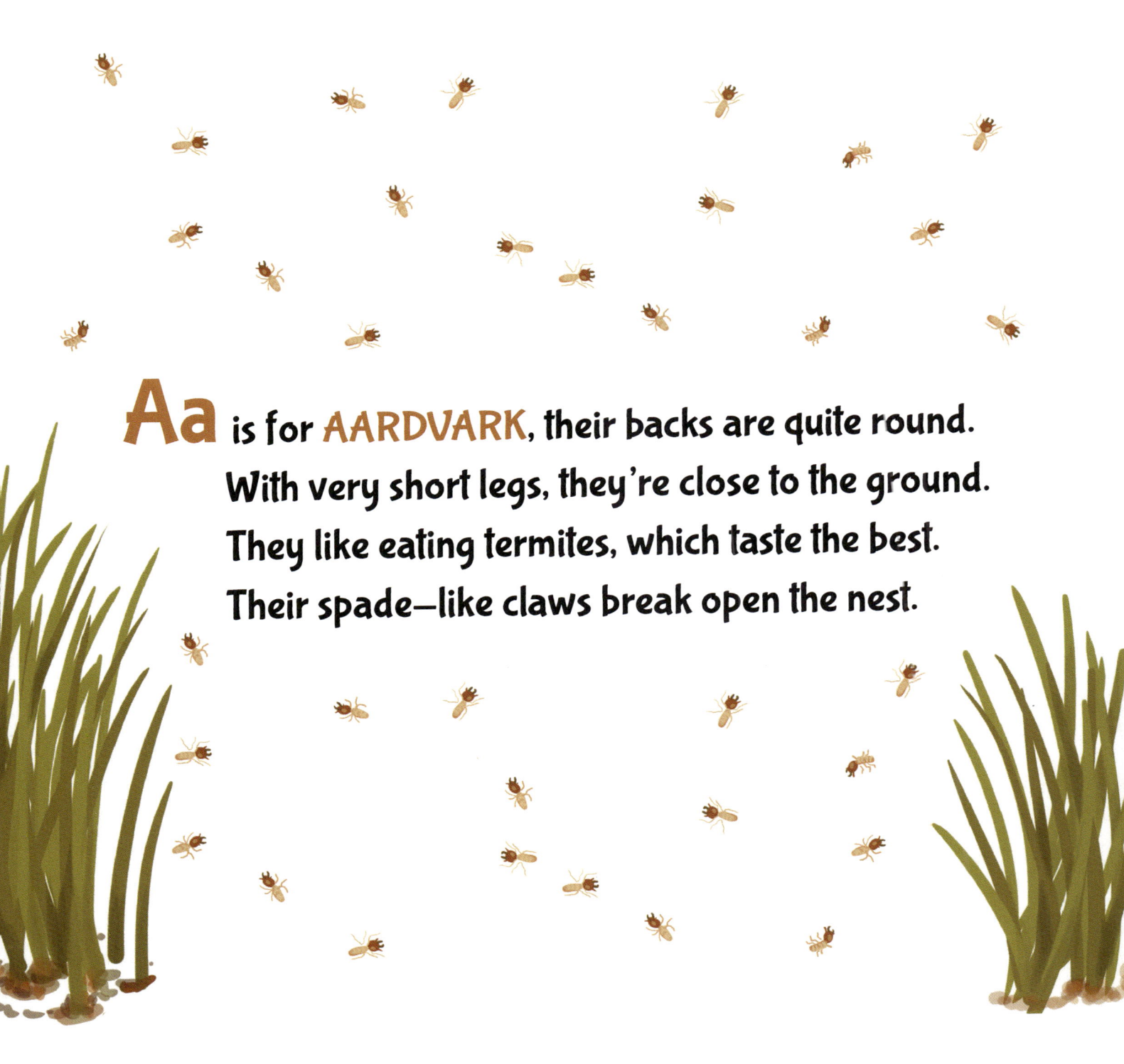

Aa is for AARDVARK, their backs are quite round.
With very short legs, they're close to the ground.
They like eating termites, which taste the best.
Their spade–like claws break open the nest.

Bb is for **BEAR**; keep away as a rule.
They look very cuddly, but don't you be fooled.
There are sun bears, black bears, pandas and more.
The grizzly and polar have a very loud roar!

Cc is for **CAMEL**. I love their big hump.
You best hold on tight going over a bump.
They live in the desert with one hump or two.
You can actually ride one... Would you like to?

Dd is for DHOLE, a wild dog so rare.
Just 2,000 left, we must be aware.
Be careful of lands that they call their home.
And give them some space: they need room to roam.

Ee is for ELEPHANT, who swings a large trunk.
It sucks up the water. It acts like a pump.
They walk quietly, and don't see that well.
They need other senses, especially their smell.

Ff is for **FOX**, so nimble and fast.
His fur so beautiful as he runs past.
Just like your cat, his claws can retract.
Don't you find that an interesting fact?

Gg is for GIRAFFE; he stretches so high!
With long legs and neck, reach up to the sky.
He doesn't drink often, because it's too hard.
Can sleep standing up, to be on his guard.

Hh is for HYENA, they make funny sounds.
They're not the prettiest animal we found.
With strong jaws and teeth, they take quite a bite.
Four different kinds, and one type has stripes.

Ii is for **IMPALA**; they travel in herds.
Find them in Africa, amongst many birds.
They bounce all around, jumping and leaping.
Confusing the enemy aids their safekeeping.

Jj is for JAGUAR, unless he is black.
Then he's a panther. Watch out: he'll attack!
He is very sleek and covered in spots.
A powerful swimmer, don't want to get caught!

Kk is for **KANGAROO**, with a strong tail and hop.
A pouch for their babies, along they will bop.
They like to eat plants, leaves, shoots and twigs.
They bound everywhere, on feet that are big!

Ll is for **LYNX**. He has thick cheek ruffs,
   Extremely large feet, and short dark ear tufts.
   They hunt in the night, they like to go see
   What prey is below by climbing in trees.

Mm is for **MOOSE**, he stands up quite tall.
He looks a bit awkward, as though he might fall.
A powerful swimmer, he can dive quite deep.
And he likes the water; cools him from the heat.

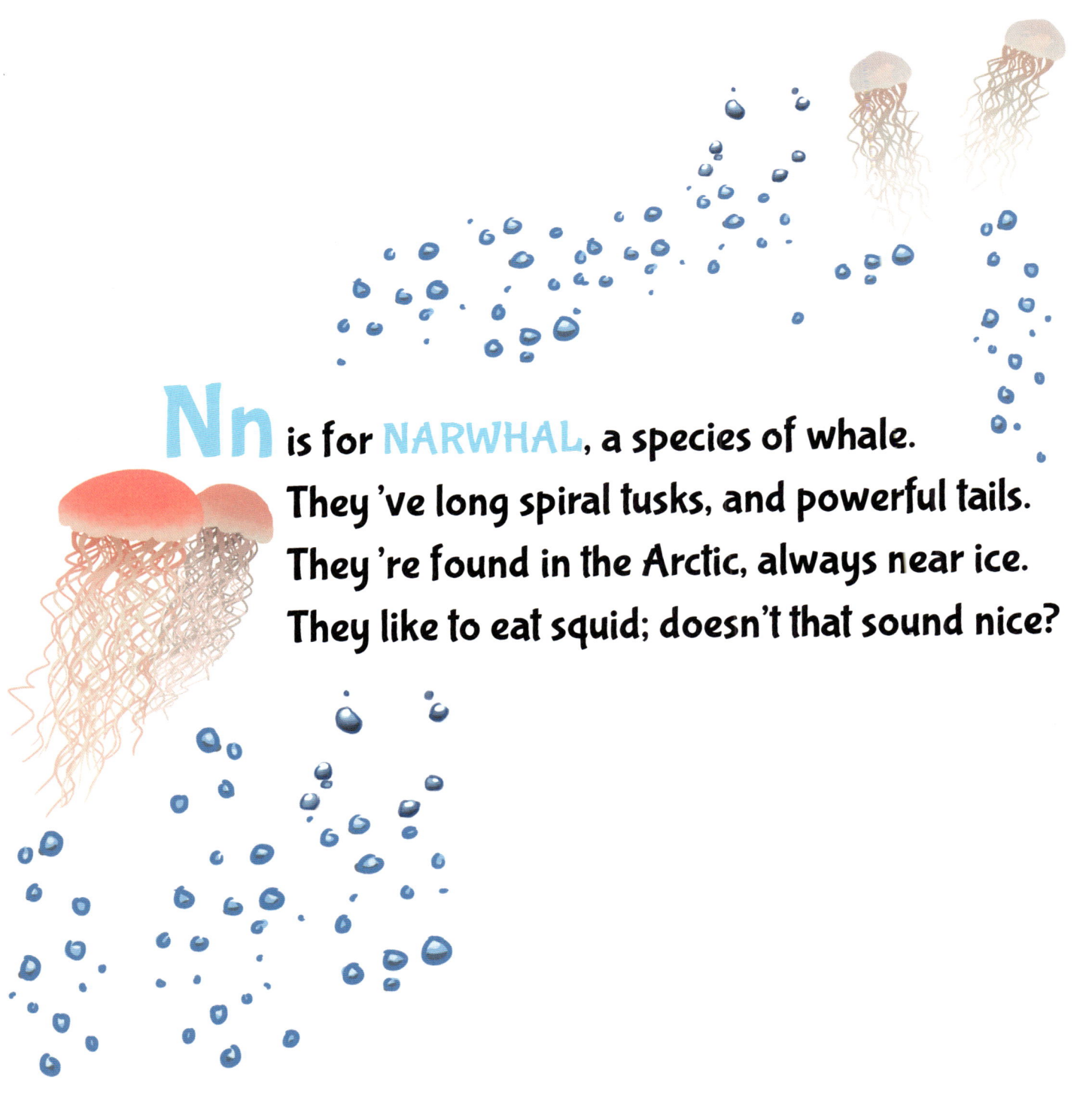

Nn is for NARWHAL, a species of whale.
They've long spiral tusks, and powerful tails.
They're found in the Arctic, always near ice.
They like to eat squid; doesn't that sound nice?

Oo is for ORANGUTAN, his shaggy hair reddish brown.
With very long arms that hang to the ground.
Most of their time is spent in the trees.
They eat lots of fruit, along with young leaves.

Pp is for **PENGUIN**, an unusual bird.
Not able to fly, that does seem absurd.
They live where it's cold, they huddle together.
By forming a circle, helps protect from weather.

Qq is for **QUAGGA**; he's no longer here.
Somewhat like a zebra, had very small ears.
Had dark brownish stripes, on his neck and head.
They grazed on the grasses, that's how they fed.

Rr is for RHINOCEROS, they weigh more than a ton.
They have two sharp horns, on short legs they run.
Their sight is not good, but they can hear and smell.
And with their big horn, they dig bulbs up well.

Ss is for SLOTH, he's the slowest of slow.
He hangs from the trees, there's nowhere to go.
He sleeps all day long, stays up in the night.
He hangs upside down, and that's quite a sight.

Tt is for TAPIR, has a flexible snout.
He feeds twice a day, that's when he comes out.
They like the dense forest, or large grassy plains.
And might run to water, if enemies came.

Uu is for URUS, an extinct type of ox.
Shaggy and long horned, walked carefully on rocks.
They roamed around Europe, but cannot be found.
Because they're extinct, they're no longer around.

Vv is for **VICUÑA**, they run fast and are slim.
With strange mane and teeth, long neck and limbs.
Somewhat like a llama, but with orange–red fur.
They eat short grasses and roam in small herds.

Ww is for **WARTHOG**, he is a wild pig.
He has a wide head, he is fairly big.
His long tail is tufted, his neck is quite short.
Has two pairs of tusks and makes a loud snort.

Xx is for XENOPUS, a frog with long claws.
But no tongue or teeth, I guess he can't gnaw.
Has front unwebbed fingers, his back have clawed toes.
He lives in the water, away from his foes.

Yy is for YAK, they have long shaggy hair.
Live high in the mountains, where air is more rare.
They are very smart, and easily tamed.
Can carry large packs, because they've been trained.

Zz is for ZEBRA, looks like a small horse.
Their body has stripes, that's different of course.
They run as a herd, a collection of stripes.
An enemy chasing is confused by the sight.

Aa Bb Cc Dd Ee Ff Gg Hh Ii Jj Kk Ll Mm

These are the letters in our alphabet.

And so many animals, we have finally met.

I like to learn things and read it in rhyme.

Let's do it again, please! Just one more time!

Nn Oo Pp Qq Rr Ss Tt Uu Vv Ww Xx Yy Zz

CPSIA information can be obtained
at www.ICGtesting.com
Printed in the USA
LVIC05n0740191214
419498LV00007B/24